Date: 7/29/21

J BIO JENNER
Schwartz, Heather E.,
Kylie Jenner : makeup mogul

ALTERNATOR
BOOKS™

KYLIE JENNER

MAKEUP
MOGUL

HEATHER E. SCHWARTZ

Lerner Publications ◆ Minneapolis

Lerner Publications Company
An imprint of Lerner Publishing Group, Inc.
241 First Avenue North
Minneapolis, MN 55401 USA

For reading levels and more information, look up this title at www.lernerbooks.com.

Main body text set in Aptifer Sans LT Pro.
Typeface provided by Linotype AG.

Editor: Alison Lorenz **Designer:** Lindsey Owens **Photo Editor:** Rebecca Higgins

Library of Congress Cataloging-in-Publication Data

Names: Schwartz, Heather E., author.
Title: Kylie Jenner : makeup mogul / Heather E. Schwartz.
Description: Minneapolis : Lerner Publications, 2021. | Series: Boss lady bios
    (alternator books) | Includes bibliographical references and index. | Audience:
    Ages 8–12 | Audience: Grades K–1 | Summary: "At twenty-two, Kylie Jenner is a
    makeup mogul, a mother, and an anti-bullying advocate. But she has been a
    household name since she was nine. Follow her journey from young reality star
    to successful tycoon." —Provided by publisher.
Identifiers: LCCN 2019039935 (print) | LCCN 2019039936 (ebook) |
    ISBN 9781541597099 (library binding) | ISBN 9781541599680 (ebook)
Subjects: LCSH: Jenner, Kylie—Juvenile literature. | Television personalities—
    United States—Biography—Juvenile literature. | Celebrities—United States—
    Biography—Juvenile literature. | Businesspeople—United States—Biography—
    Juvenile literature.
Classification: LCC PN1992.4.J48 S39 2020 (print) | LCC PN1992.4.J48 (ebook) |
    DDC 791.4502/8092 [B]—dc23

LC record available at https://lccn.loc.gov/2019039935
LC ebook record available at https://lccn.loc.gov/2019039936

Manufactured in the United States of America
1-47813-48253-12/30/2019

TABLE OF CONTENTS

Kylie Jenner meets with fans at a Kylie Cosmetics product launch in 2018.

LAUNCH PARTY

ON MAY 22, 2019, KYLIE JENNER LAUNCHED KYLIE SKIN, HER NEW CRUELTY-FREE, VEGAN SKIN CARE LINE. Within minutes, her products sold out. She was ready to celebrate—big time.

Dressed in a strapless pink minidress covered with crystals, Jenner took to the roller-skating rink screaming with laughter.

Guests skated around her to the pumping beats of songs by Jennifer Lopez and Jenner's boyfriend, Travis Scott. Others enjoyed glittery ice-cream cones and sushi wrapped in pink rice. Everyone was there to support Jenner and revel in her latest success.

Just a few days earlier, Jenner had posted on Instagram. "Building my makeup line from the ground up has taught me a lot, and I'm so blessed with that knowledge to apply to my brand new company," she wrote. "I've been working on this for what feels like a lifetime."

Jenner builds her company with the help of her huge social media following.

CHAPTER 1

GROWING UP ON CAMERA

Producer Ryan Seacrest (*far left*), Kylie (*front center*), and her big family at the premiere of *Keeping Up with the Kardashians*

KYLIE JENNER WAS BORN ON AUGUST 10, 1997, TO HER PARENTS, CAITLYN AND KRIS JENNER.
Caitlyn Jenner had been a famous Olympic athlete, while Kris Jenner managed the former athlete's career. The family lived in Los Angeles, and Kylie was the youngest child. Growing up, she had plenty of siblings to keep her company.

She had her sister Kendall and eight half siblings: Kourtney, Kim, Khloe, and Rob Kardashian, and Burt, Brandon, Brody, and Casey Jenner.

When Kylie was nine, famous producer Ryan Seacrest was looking to cast a new reality TV show. He thought the Kardashian-Jenner clan might be perfect. He sent a camera operator to capture them at a family barbecue and loved their energy. With that, *Keeping Up with the Kardashians* was born. The show premiered in 2007.

Kylie (*right*) and her sister Kendall in 2007

As a reality TV star, Kylie grew up with the whole world watching. When she tried new makeup, argued with her siblings, or worried about her parents' marriage, viewers were there with her. The show quickly gained millions of fans. Her siblings began modeling, taking movie roles, and building different businesses.

Kylie (*center left*) attends the Teen Choice Awards in 2010.

Kylie (*left*) and Kendall at a movie premiere in 2010

Being part of a famous family had its benefits. In 2010, when Kylie was thirteen, Sears asked her to start modeling for them. The next year, the family worked with the brand OPI to create a nail polish line called Kardashian Kolors. Kylie got to name two colors: "Wear Something Spar-Kylie" and "Rainbow in the S-Kylie."

Kylie was rich and famous, but she still had a lot in common with teens who didn't star on a reality show. She had a favorite school subject: English. She loved shopping. She wanted to have a boyfriend someday. Kylie didn't find the fame, fans, and financial advantages of being a star unusual.

Fourteen-year-old Kylie strikes a pose on the red carpet.

"I don't remember how it was before [I was famous] because I was nine when this all started," she said. "So it's kind of like I grew up into it. It's kind of like I don't know any different."

GETTING IT DONE!

At fourteen, Kylie had 1.3 million followers on Twitter.

YOU'RE THE BOSS

You don't have to be famous to find opportunities. Thanks to the internet, anyone can star on a YouTube channel. You could focus on fashion, makeup, a favorite school subject, or anything else you're passionate about: music, sports, movies, or whatever you like!

As your show's producer, you get total control. Besides what you *should* keep private for safety reasons—such as your school and your home address—you can decide what you *want* to keep private. As the star, you get to voice your opinions and share what you know. You can even curate your audience, making videos private and inviting only family and friends to watch.

CHAPTER 2
LIFE IN THE SPOTLIGHT

Kylie (*left*) and Kendall with their *Seventeen* magazine cover in 2012

IN 2012 KYLIE AND HER SISTER KENDALL APPEARED ON THE COVER OF *TEEN VOGUE* MAGAZINE. The accompanying article said Kylie's enormous closet was full of shoes, jewelry, purses, and more. It was enough to make any reader envy her.

But the article also described the difficulties of living in the spotlight. Kylie and her family had almost no privacy. When paparazzi spotted Kylie walking with pop singer Cody Simpson, the media reported that they were dating. It could be embarrassing when strangers scrutinized private moments.

Her family's fame meant cameras followed Kylie everywhere.

Kylie wore dark lipstick to the American Music Awards in 2014.

Around 2014 Kylie began getting attention for her looks—specifically, her plump lips. When fans speculated that she'd had plastic surgery, she fought back, tweeting that her feelings were hurt.

When Kylie made *Time* magazine's Most Influential Teens list in October 2014, more mean comments came her way. Some people didn't believe she belonged on the list alongside education activist Malala Yousafzai and presidential daughter Malia Obama.

But Kylie knew she was setting trends and influencing people in her own way. This time, she ignored her critics. "I didn't care what people had to say. I didn't even read any of that stuff," she said.

Kylie takes a selfie in 2015.

"BE KIND TO EVERYBODY . . . [DON'T] MAKE IT ABOUT YOU. GET OUT THERE, DO SOMETHING, AND HELP PEOPLE."

Kylie and Caitlyn Jenner at the 2015 *Glamour* Women of the Year Awards

Late in 2014, Kylie's parents divorced. They continued to have a friendly relationship and worked to make a tough situation easier on their kids. The following year, the family went through another change. Caitlyn Jenner, who was assigned male at birth, came out as a transgender woman. The shift and her family's reactions played out on TV for all to see. But Kylie was used to that. She and her family would work things out in the public eye, the way they always had.

Kylie's fans love her signature lip look.

CHAPTER 3
TAKING CONTROL

IN 2015 SOME OF JENNER'S FANS TRIED TO COPY HER FULL LIPS IN A DANGEROUS WAY. They would put their lips into a small glass and suck them to create a swollen appearance. The trend even had a catchy name: the Kylie Jenner Lip Challenge. But the challenge caused bruising and other damage. Doctors warned people to stop. At first, Jenner responded with a tweet to try to curb the trend.

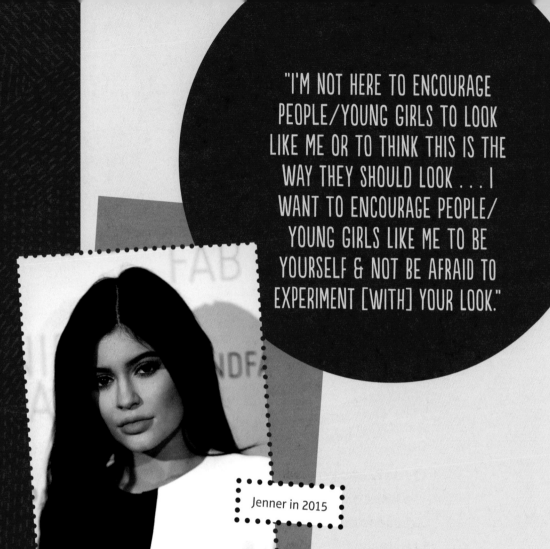

"I'M NOT HERE TO ENCOURAGE PEOPLE/YOUNG GIRLS TO LOOK LIKE ME OR TO THINK THIS IS THE WAY THEY SHOULD LOOK . . . I WANT TO ENCOURAGE PEOPLE/ YOUNG GIRLS LIKE ME TO BE YOURSELF & NOT BE AFRAID TO EXPERIMENT [WITH] YOUR LOOK."

Jenner in 2015

Soon after, Jenner admitted to using temporary lip fillers. She said she got the fillers because she felt insecure about her lips. Some people were angry. They hopped online to call Jenner a fake, a bad role model, and even a loser. She'd made a simple, personal decision. But because she was a reality star, people felt they had the right to judge her.

Jenner decided to harness her star power to fight bullying. Calling her campaign #IAmMoreThan, she posted six different people's stories about how they'd been bullied and invited her fans to join the conversation. The campaign celebrated different body types, sexual identities, and more.

GETTING IT DONE!

In 2015 Jenner had 34.6 million Instagram followers. That year she posted 960 pictures and received more than one billion likes.

Later that year, Jenner made *Time* magazine's Most Influential Teens list again. This time, she felt more grounded. She owned her own home and planned to launch a makeup line. The line capitalized on people's interest in her plumped-up lip look. Jenner invested her own money in the company and used Instagram to tell her many followers what was coming. When she released the Kylie Lip Kit in November 2015, her fan base was eager to buy. In less than two years, her company earned $420 million in sales.

Jenner looks over her Lip Kits in 2018.

Kylie Cosmetics, Jenner's makeup company, earned millions of dollars in just a few years.

CHAPTER 4
FINDING BALANCE

IN 2016 JENNER RENAMED HER COMPANY KYLIE COSMETICS. The company quickly gained its own following, earning 10.2 million Instagram followers by the end of the year. That year *Forbes* magazine ranked Jenner second on its Top-Earning Reality Stars list. She earned $18 million total from her company, her family's reality show, and endorsement deals

Jenner is involved in every aspect of Kylie Cosmetics, from marketing to product design.

with companies including Puma, PacSun, and Topshop. She outranked her sisters Kourtney, Khloe, and Kendall, and her mother, Kris.

As a business owner, Jenner had a busy schedule. She got up each day and checked incoming orders to see which products were selling the fastest. She met with her manufacturer about new products they were developing together. Jenner also thought constantly about what she wanted to offer her fans.

Everything about her business mattered to her, from the smell of her lipsticks to the look of her Kylie Cosmetics web page.

But Jenner had more on her mind than money. She had a lot going on in her personal life too. In 2017 she met rapper Travis Scott. Soon she decided to go on tour with him. Traveling to different cities, they were able to get to know each other away from the prying eyes of fans and paparazzi. They became a serious couple.

Jenner (*right*) and Scott at a basketball game in 2018

Scott and Jenner hold their daughter, Stormi, in 2019.

The next year, Jenner and Scott had a daughter together. They named her Stormi Webster (Webster is Scott's real last name). Jenner had successfully kept her pregnancy a secret, and her daughter's birth surprised fans. On Instagram, Jenner explained her need for the privacy. While she loved sharing her life with her fans, she knew that staying out of the public eye during her pregnancy was the healthiest choice for her.

Balancing her private life and public image took work, but Jenner was up for the challenge. She continued to work on growing her brand. Capitalizing on her huge social media following, she spent hours posting pictures of herself wearing her products on Instagram and Snapchat. She created professional shots, finding the best lighting to display her products. She also posted videos and announced new launches. In 2018 she made *Forbes*'s list of richest self-made women, ranking number 27 with her net worth estimated at $900 million.

Kylie Cosmetics' Lip Kits remain among the brand's top-selling products.

In March 2019, *Forbes* named the twenty-one-year-old Jenner the youngest-ever self-made billionaire. Jenner rolled out Kylie Skin a few months later. She plans to keep growing the business she loves and giving her fans what they want.

Jenner went for a bold look at the Met Gala in 2019.

GETTING IT DONE!

When Jenner launched Kylie Skin in May 2019, some products sold out within minutes.

Jenner in 2019

"It's incredible to be recognized for something I'm so passionate about, and I'm really grateful for that," she said. "Connecting with my fans and creating product that excites them has been an incredible process. I've learned so much along the way and I hope to inspire others to follow their dreams."

TIMELINE

1997   Kylie Jenner is born in Los Angeles on August 10.

2007   *Keeping Up with the Kardashians* premieres.

2012   Kylie and her sister Kendall appear on the cover of *Teen Vogue*.

2014   The Kylie Jenner Lip Challenge becomes popular.

2015   Jenner appears on *Time* magazine's Most Influential Teens list for the second time.

         She launches the Kylie Lip Kit, her first makeup product.

2016   She renames her company Kylie Cosmetics.

2017   She begins dating rapper Travis Scott.

2018   She makes *Forbes*'s list of richest self-made women.

         She and Scott have a daughter, Stormi.

2019   She is named the world's youngest self-made billionaire by *Forbes* magazine.

GLOSSARY

brand: a category of products that are all made by one company and all have a specific name or look

capitalize: to use to achieve certain ends, such as making money

curate: to organize and select according to certain standards

endorsement: a public or official statement of support or approval

net worth: the total value of a person's assets

paparazzi: photographers who follow famous people around to take pictures to sell to magazines and newspapers

premiere: to play publicly for the first time

producer: someone who is in charge of making and, usually, providing money for a play, movie, or album

scrutinize: to examine carefully in a critical way

trend: something that is popular at a certain moment in time

SOURCE NOTES

5   Anna Starostinetskaya, "Kylie Jenner Debuts Vegan Skincare Line," *VegNews*, May 14, 2019.

10   Sarah Crow, "Kylie Jenner Reveals Her Latest Ambition: Acting!," *Wetpaint*, November 15, 2013, http://www.wetpaint.com/kylie-jenner-wants-to -act-794341/.

15   Daniel D'Addario, "Kylie Jenner: I Want to Be 'an Inspiration for Young Girls,'" *Time*, October 29, 2015, https://time.com/4087040/kylie-jenner-interview/.

15   D'Addario.

18   Molly Mulshine, "Kylie Jenner Responds to the Out-of-Control #KylieJennerChallenge That Has Teens Suctioning Shot Glasses to Their Lips to Mimic Her Look," *Business Insider*, April 21, 2015, https://www.businessinsider.com/kylie-jenner -responds-to-shot-glass-lips-2015-4/.

27   Lisa Lockwood, "Kylie Jenner Makes Forbes List of America's Richest Self-Made Women," *WWD*, July 11, 2018, https://wwd.com/business-news/media/kylie -jenner-makes-forbes-list-of-americas-richest-self -made-women-1202752485/.

LEARN MORE

Bernhardt, Carolyn. *Snap It! Snapchat Projects for the Real World*. Minneapolis: Abdo, 2017.

Biz Kids
http://bizkids.com/

Cuban, Mark, Shaan Patel, and Ian McCue. *Kid Start-Up: How You Can Be an Entrepreneur*. New York: Diversion Books, 2018.

Kapp, Diana. *Girls Who Run the World*. New York: Delacorte Books for Young Readers, 2019.

Mattern, Joanne. *Kylie Jenner*. Hallandale, FL: Mitchell Lane, 2019.

Rusick, Jessica. *Kylie Jenner: Contemporary Cosmetics Mogul*. Minneapolis: Abdo, 2020.

TeenBusiness: Girl Bosses
http://www.teenbusiness.com/girl-bosses

Teen Vogue: Kylie Jenner Gave a YouTube Video Tour of her Kylie Cosmetics Headquarters
https://www.teenvogue.com/story/kylie-jenner-youtube -video-tour-kylie-cosmetics-headquarters

INDEX

PHOTO ACKNOWLEDGMENTS

Image credits: Rick Kern/Getty Images, pp. 4, 20; A. Mertens/Shutterstock.com, pp. 5, 25; Jeff Vespa/WireImage/Getty Images, pp. 6-7; Kevin Mazur/Getty Images, p. 8; Featureflash Photo Agency/Shutterstock.com, p. 9; Denise Truscello/WireImage/Getty Images, p. 10; Paul Archuleta/FilmMagic/Getty Images, p. 12; Christopher Polk/WireImage/Getty Images, p. 13 (left); Jon Kopaloff/FilmMagic/Getty Images, pp. 13-14; JoMichael Buckner/BMA2015/Getty Images, p. 15; Nicholas Hunt/Getty Images, p. 16; Jeff Kravitz/Getty Images, pp. 17, 22; Frazer Harrison/Getty Images, p. 18; Vivien Killilea/Getty Images, p. 19; melissamn/Shutterstock.com, p. 21; Bob Levey/Getty Images, p. 23; Jon Kopaloff/FilmMagic/Getty Images, p. 24; Kevin Tachman/Getty Images, p. 26; Gilbert Carrasquillo/Getty Images, p. 27. Design elements: kondratya/iStock/Getty Images; iakievy/DigitalVisionVectors/Getty Images; Tanyasun/iStock/Getty Images; katflare/iStock/Getty Images; mhatzapa/Shutterstock.com; Anatartan/iStock/Getty Images.

Cover: Frazer Harrison/Getty Images.